CARL MARIA VON WEBER

Great Overtures

IN FULL SCORE

Jubilee Overture, Preciosa, Der Freischütz,
Euryanthe and Oberon

DOVER PUBLICATIONS, INC.
NEW YORK

Copyright © 1986 by Dover Publications, Inc.
All rights reserved under Pan American and International Copyright Conventions.

Published in Canada by General Publishing Company, Ltd., 30 Lesmill Road, Don Mills, Toronto, Ontario.
Published in the United Kingdom by Constable and Company, Ltd., 10 Orange Street, London WC2H 7EG.

This Dover edition, first published in 1986, consists of the following:
The overture to *Preciosa* as published by Breitkopf & Härtel, Leipzig, n.d. (plate number Part.B. 1686).
The overtures to *Der Freischütz*, *Euryanthe* and *Oberon*, and the *Jubilee Overture*, as published in *Ouvertüren für Orchester von C. M. von Weber* by C. F. Peters, Leipzig, n.d. (plate number for *Der Freischütz*, 8449; for the three others, 6246).

Manufactured in the United States of America
Dover Publications, Inc., 31 East 2nd Street, Mineola, N.Y. 11501

Library of Congress Cataloging in Publication Data

Weber, Carl Maria von, 1786–1826.
  [Overtures. Selections]
  Great overtures.

  Reprint of works originally published: Leipzig : Breitkopf & Härtel, n.d. (2nd work); Leipzig : C.F. Peters, n.d. (remainder).
  Contents: Jubilee overture : composed 1818 = Jubel-Ouvertüre—Overture to the incidental music to the play Preciosa : composed 1820—Overture to the opera Der Freischütz : composed 1817–21—[etc.]
  M1004.W373G7 1986   86-752599
  ISBN 0-486-25225-6 (pbk.)

Contents

Jubilee Overture

GOD SAVE THE KING.

Overture to *Preciosa*

Zigeunermarsch nach einer echten Zigeunermelodie. (Gypsy march after an authentic Gypsy tune.)

Moderato ma tutto ben marcato.

Moderato ma tutto ben marcato.

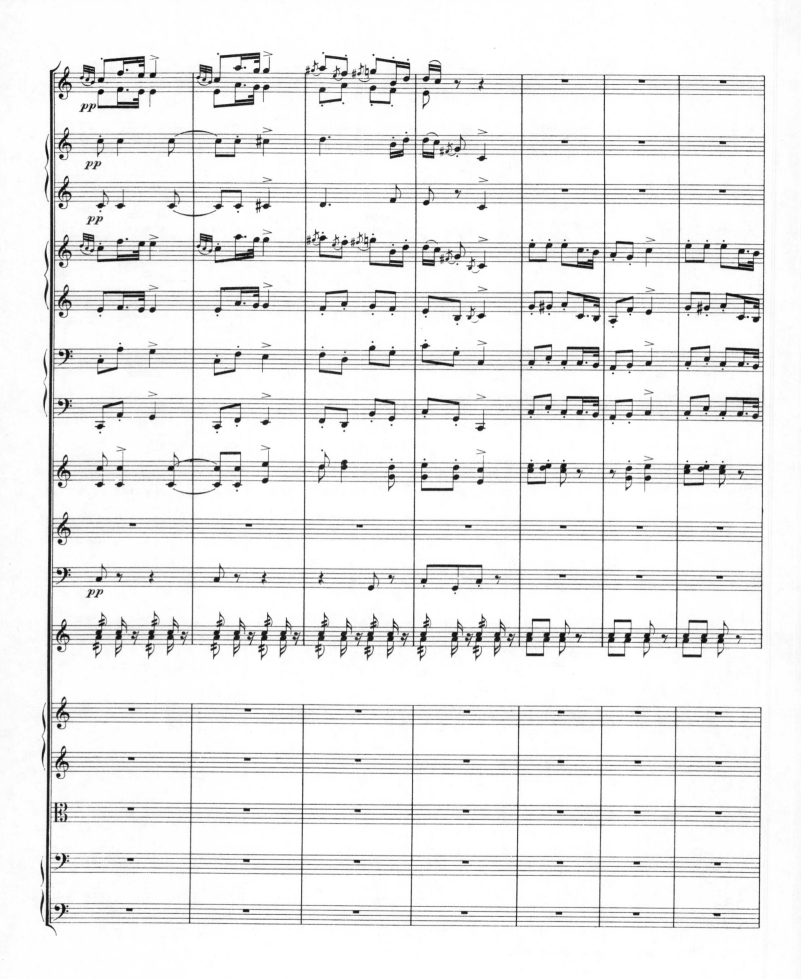

Allegro con fuoco.

Overture to *Der Freischütz*

Vcello. e Basso.

Vcello. e Basso.

Overture to *Euryanthe*

Overture to *Oberon*

Overture to *Oberon*